HOW TO MAKE CUSTOM SEWN SNEAKERS – THE COMPLETE PRODUCTION PROCESS

BY ANTHONY BOYD

Copyright © 2015 Anaghe Inc
All rights reserved.
ISBN: 9780692555743

ANTHONY BOYD

YOUR MEMBERSHIP AT WWW.ANAGHE.COM IS FREE WITH THE PURCHASE OF THIS BOOK TO REDEEM YOUR MEMBERSHIP&WATCH THE INSTRUCTIONAL VIDEOS PLEASE FOLLOW THE STEPS BELOW.

BOOK BUYERS : SIGN UP ON THE WEBSITE AND FORWARD PROOF OF PURCHASE (RECEIPT WITH CONFIRMATION #)AN APPROVAL NOTIFACATION WILL BE SENT BY EMAIL WITH IN 24 HRS.

NEW MEMBERS : MAKE MEMBERSHIP PAYMENT FOR EBOOK DOWNLOAD &

VIDEO ACCESS THEN SIGN UP ON THE SITE FOR YOUR APPROVAL NOTIFACATION ALLOW UP TO 24 HRS FOR PROCESSING.

HOW TO MAKE CUSTOM SEWN SNEAKERS -THE COMPLETE PRODUCTION PROCESS

BY ANTHONY BOYD
Copyright

2015 by
Anaghe Inc.

All rights reserved. Written permission must be secured from the publisher to use or reproduce any part of this book, except for brief quotations in critical reviews or articles.
WWW.ANAGHE.COM
https://www.youtube.com/user/AnagheInc

ANTHONY BOYD

TABLE OF CONTENTS

CHAPTER 1: THE FOUNDATION 5

CHAPTER 2: GRIP REMOVAL................................7

CHAPTER 3: THE BREAKDOWN 10

CHAPTER 4: THE COVERING 13

CHAPTER 4A: FIRST PREPARATION 20

CHAPTER 5: THE RECONSTRUCTION 21

CHAPTER 6: REBUILDING THE FOUNDATION ... 56

CHAPTER 7: SECOND PREPARATION.................. 78

CHAPTER 8: REATTACHING THE GRIP 80

Introduction

My interest in customizing sneakers began in grade school and grew into a business by my adult years. I went from Sharpies to acrylic paint to partial breakdowns to full ones. And through the years I found one thing remained supreme in this world of sneaker heads. "You ain't got these!" and the reaction from onlookers and admirers made the hard work well worth it, not to mention the profit generated. This underground Sneaker thing of ours that grew out of Hip Hop has produced and developed artists and businessmen from all walks of life to address the needs of the modern B-Boy.

It answers the call of a shoe craftsman whose trade is being lost in the shuffle of mass consumption. It is my honor to pass on years of know how to worthy individuals to ensure that the craft of shoe making lives and thrives in the world and business of Hip Hop. Please keep in mind that this is an art and that it may take years to develop all the skills necessary, such as sewing with an industrial machine, pattern creation and manipulation, grip removal, etc All these skills will grow with time as you master the basics of reconstruction outlined in this book. Your familiarity will increase as you complete each step and eventually you'll be able to replace parts of the shoe, if not all of it, with new fabrics and interfacing. Lastly, I'd like to dedicate this book to my son Kaylen Anaghe Boyd, Rest in Peace, and to Dapper Dan, the first to design and produce custom clothing, custom footwear , custom car exteriors and interiors for the STREETS years before there was a so-called urban clothing market. Check for his work on any 80's Hip Hop artist or D-boy that came out of that era.

HOW TO MAKE CUSTOM SEWN SNEAKERS

Chapter 1:
The Foundation

SHOE LAST

A last is a mechanical form that has a shape similar to that of a human foot.

It is used by shoemakers and cordwainers in the manufacture and repair of shoes.

Lasts typically come in pairs and have been made from various materials, including hardwoods, cast iron, and high-density plastics.

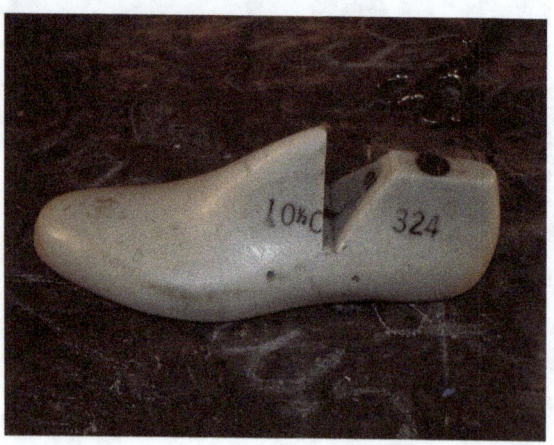

This tool will be used to stabilize, shape and in some cases reform the sneaker, as well as assist in reattaching the under and outer sole. The selection of the proper last is critical because this is the foundation of the sneaker shape, so pay careful attention to the toe region of the last. As most sneakers are rounded at the toe, your last must reflect this roundedness also. The cost could range from $100 to $500 a pair new, or $50 to $250 a pair used.

Chapter 2:
Grip Removal

HEAT GUN

A heat gun is a device used to emit a stream of hot air, usually at temperatures between 100°C and 550°C (200-1000°F), with some hotter models running around 760°C (1400°F), which can be held by hand. Heat guns usually have the form of an elongated body pointing at what is to be heated, with a handle fixed to it at right angles and a trigger, in the same general layout as a handgun, hence the name.

This tool will be used to remove the grip. As we all know, heat is the biggest reason for sole separation. This device will help speed up that process and enable you to loosen the membranes in the glue. First, score around the grip with a razor where it meets with the leather; only score, not cut into,

Then apply heat to the toe area, being careful not to burn or melt the rubber. Once heated enough to hold,

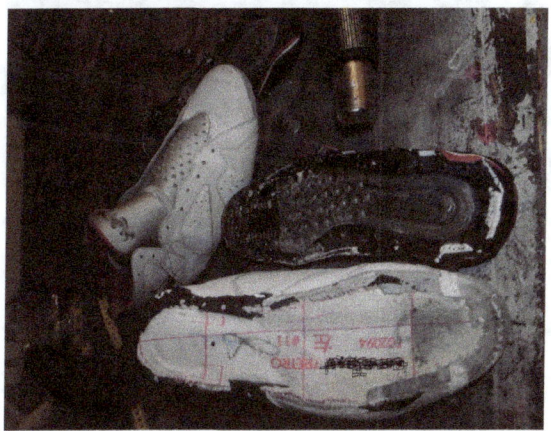

use a butter knife to pry the grip away from the leather on the heated areas only. Pull when

HOW TO MAKE CUSTOM SEWN SNEAKERS

needed, but gently or you may pull away portions of the grip. Repeat this process till the grip is completely removed, keeping in mind to loosen the sides first and then the bottom.

After you have removed the grip you may have to remove parts of the grip (rubber) from the sneaker. You can sand or melt it away. It doesn't all have to be removed, just enough so the surface is flat.

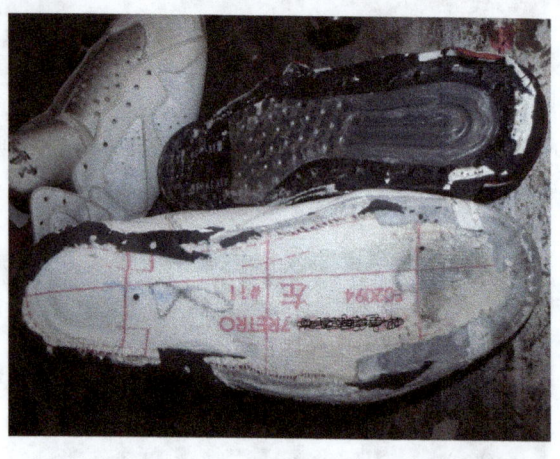

***

Chapter 3:
The Breakdown

RAZOR

This tool will be used to break or cut the stitches used to construct the sneaker. The thinness of the blade will allow you to slide it between seams with ease but be sure to purchase a one-sided blade, for you will need the extra pressure applied with your finger to cut through. Begin popping the stitches on the sole taround the toe, and work your way back.

After you have taken the sneaker completely

HOW TO MAKE CUSTOM SEWN SNEAKERS

apart, make sure you have all the pieces you intend to cover or replace. Then mark only one shoe with an X so you know your right from your left during the production process.

Sneaker

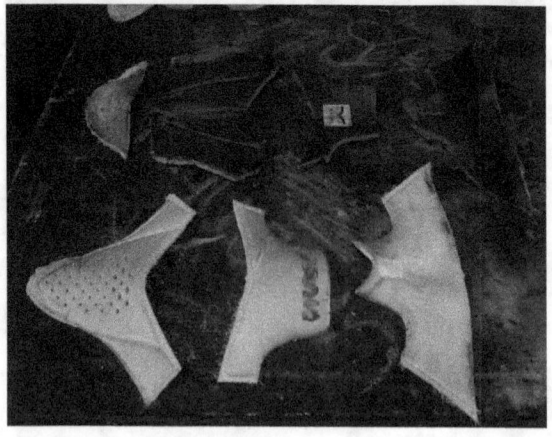

ANTHONY BOYD

Liner

Interfacing

Chapter 4:
The Covering

SPRAY ADHESIVE

A spray adhesive is any substance applied to the surfaces of materials that binds them together and resists separation. Any kind of glue spray will do because several coats will be applied to ensure the permanent bonding of the leathers, which brings me to material selection. When selecting hides, your main concern is thickness. You want thin and pliable fabrics to ensure a sleek finish. Thicker hides can be used but only as replacement pattern pieces.

First lay out the sneaker pieces you wish to cover on newspaper for quick clean up,

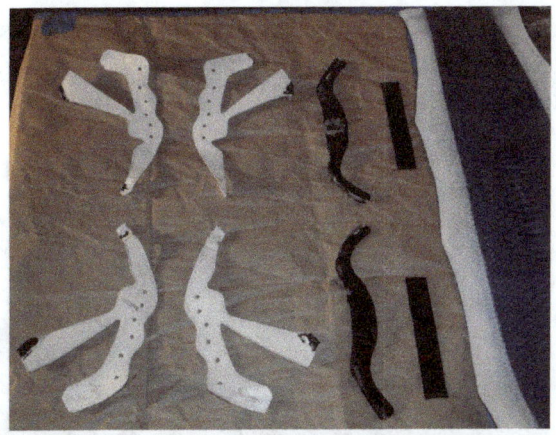

then add 3 to 5 coats to the pieces, being sure to apply evenly and allowing partial dryness between coats. Second, lay your hides out with finish side down so the back of the hide is facing up.

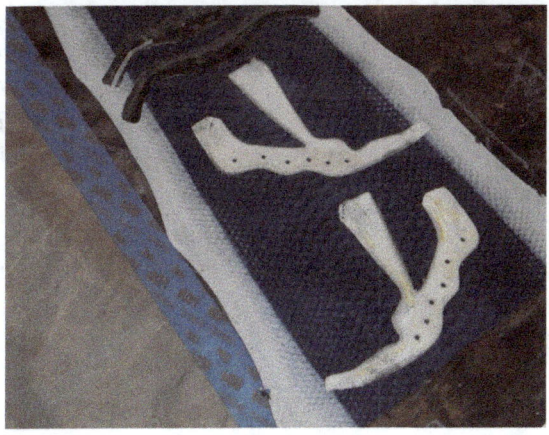

Then take the sprayed sneaker pieces and place

HOW TO MAKE CUSTOM SEWN SNEAKERS

them on the hides with enough space between them for seam allowance to fold over the edges of the sneaker pieces.

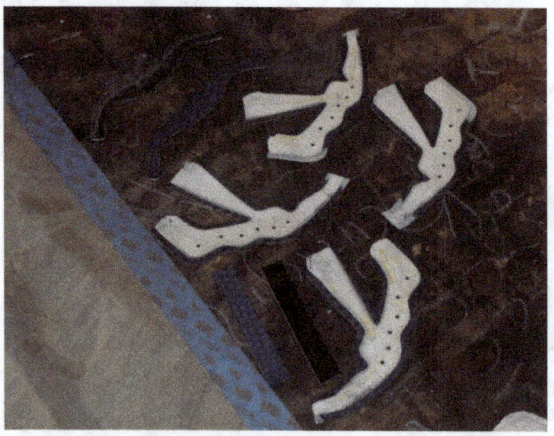

Press firmly to ensure an even bond.

Third, cut out your sneaker pieces as stated above, with a small seam allowance to fold over .Now place these pieces on fresh newspaper with the finished side down and spray 1 to 2 coats of glue around the seam allowance, then begin to fold it over the edges, creating notches/clips as you go in the curved areas to ensure the fabric lies flat around the edge.

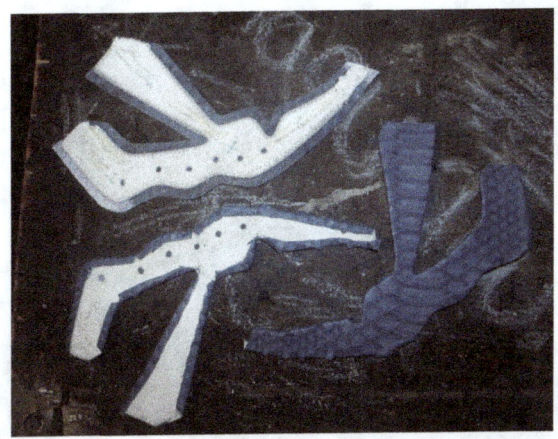

Repeat the process above for the remaining pieces you wish to cover, keeping in mind that you may not have a need to fold over the edges of some pieces first because it may not show, or because it's part of your design.

HOW TO MAKE CUSTOM SEWN SNEAKERS

ANTHONY BOYD

Sneaker Covered

HOW TO MAKE CUSTOM SEWN SNEAKERS

Liner Covered

Chapter 4a:
First Preparation

This is where you would begin to apply logos and the design elements you wish. I would suggest punching your first set of holes for the laces because it helps greatly with lining up the pieces for sewing and at this stage you have the mobility to work on certain parts of the sneaker that you wouldn't have if it were together. Here you can also begin to restyle the grip by painting or covering certain parts.

Chapter 5:
The Reconstruction

SEWING MACHINE

A sewing machine is a machine used to stitch fabric and other materials together with thread. Sewing skills are needed in this section to ensure a clean finish. I recommend that you practice with scrap materials and become familiar with the machine before you begin your project because you only have ONE shot. Leather stitches that may have to be removed will leave holes from the needle punching. But before we get into the sewing portion let's discuss machine selection.

The Type of Machine Needed

These processes can't be done on a home sewing machine; it must be an industrial machine with a table and motor. A single needle straight stitch,

a walking foot single needle straight stitch,

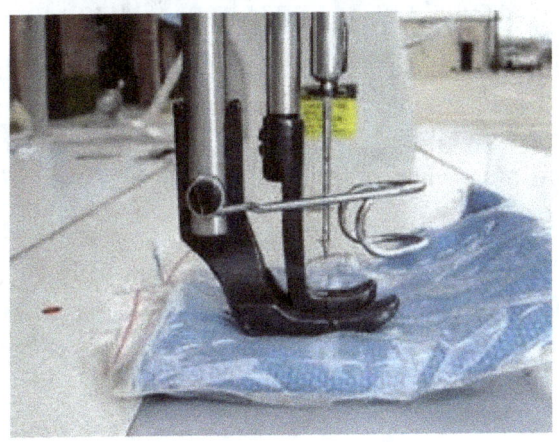

or a post bed single needle straight stitch

HOW TO MAKE CUSTOM SEWN SNEAKERS

will do to achieve a nice clean finish. These machines could range in price from $200 to $1500.

Since straight stitch single needle machines are more accessible and affordable, the production process will be based on this machinery and we will note when other machines can be used in a process.

When I say clean finish this means no skipped or loose stitches, all stitches the same length and straight.

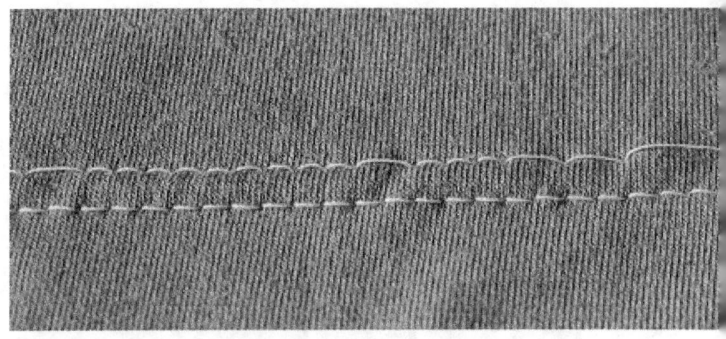

To achieve this, practice and make adjustments to your machine to prevent loose and skipped stitches. As to your sewing skills, they can only be improved with sewing drills and time.

SEWING DRILLS

1. Draw a straight line on a piece of fabric and sew on the line.

HOW TO MAKE CUSTOM SEWN SNEAKERS

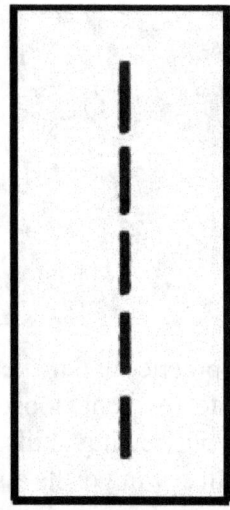

2. Draw a circle on a piece of fabric and sew on the line.

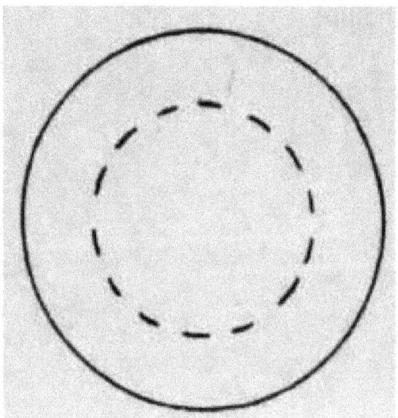

3. Draw a squiggly line on a piece of fabric and

sew on the line.

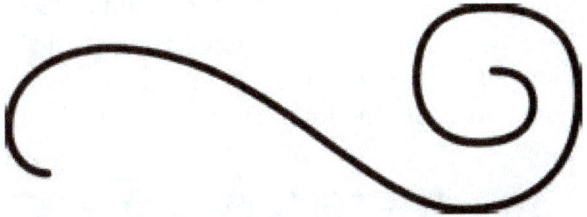

When you can sew these objects with ease and in a timely manner plus meet all the above requirements as to loose, skipped, and straight stitches, you will have increased your sewing skills greatly and are now ready to complete your project.

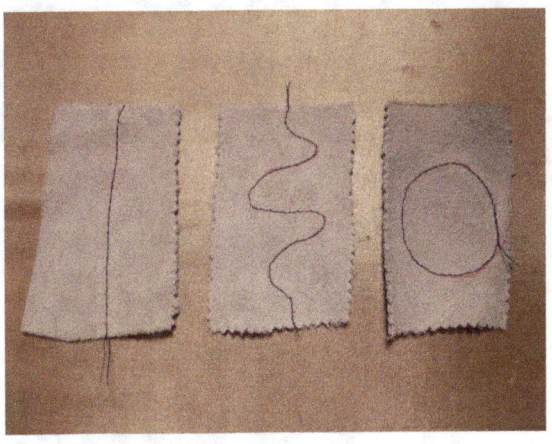

CONSTRUCTION PROCESS

First, rebuild any pieces that need to be made whole (use the stitch holes to realign the pieces).

HOW TO MAKE CUSTOM SEWN SNEAKERS

1a. First attach the toe box to the inner and outer sides. Usually this would be done with a zigzag stitch but we will create the stitch with 3 to 4 stay stitches in one place using a straight stitch machine. Don't cut the thread as you sew down the seam.

1b. Attach the interfacing to the ankle upper along with ankle cushions between and sew around the edges.

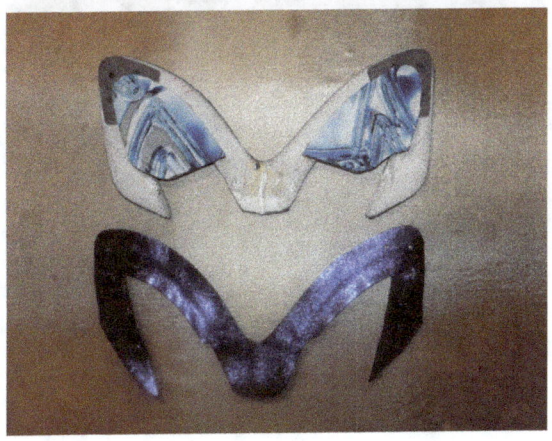

HOW TO MAKE CUSTOM SEWN SNEAKERS

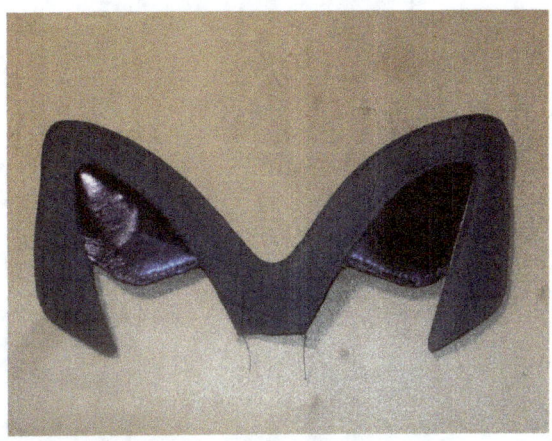

1c. Attach the heel box to the heel insert and re-glue the interfacing to the upper heel trim; then sew it in place.

HOW TO MAKE CUSTOM SEWN SNEAKERS

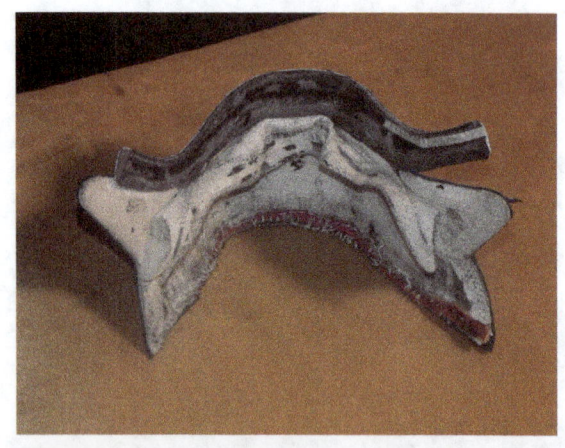

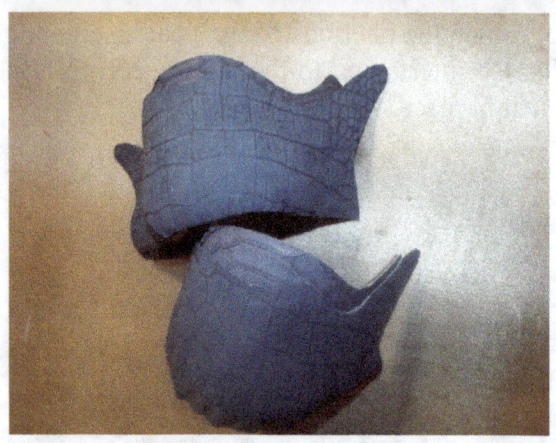

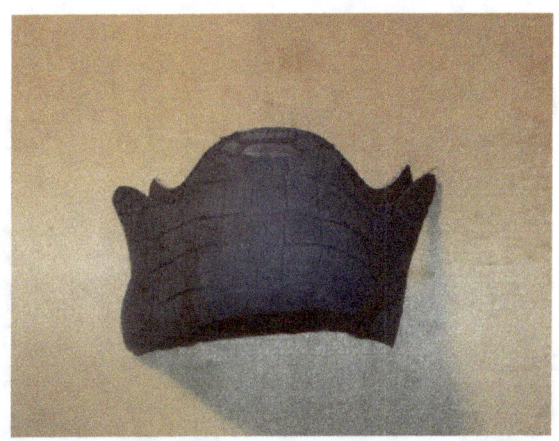

1d. Attach the heel box to the upper ankle cushions, the back of it only, and sew it in place.

HOW TO MAKE CUSTOM SEWN SNEAKERS

Sew the W-shaped pattern onto the inner and outer sides with the interfacing attached under. Then make a leather interfacing and place it over the lace hole area on the interfacing, then stitch it in place by adding a second stitch line on the other side; then re-punch the lace holes.

ANTHONY BOYD

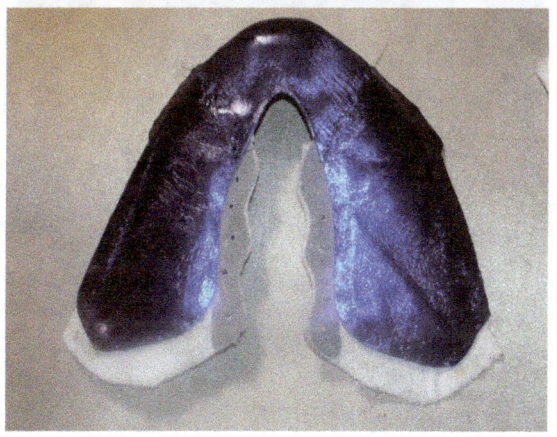

HOW TO MAKE CUSTOM SEWN SNEAKERS

ANTHONY BOYD

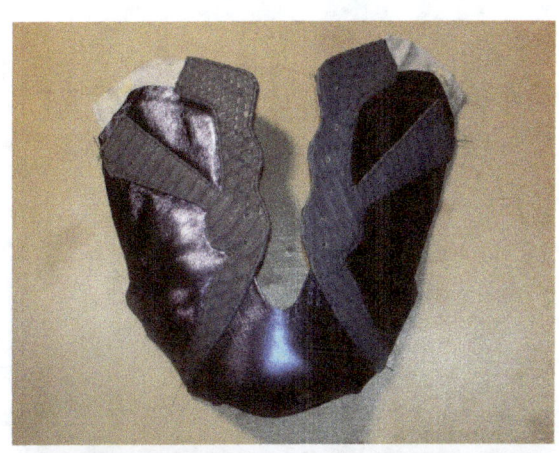

HOW TO MAKE CUSTOM SEWN SNEAKERS

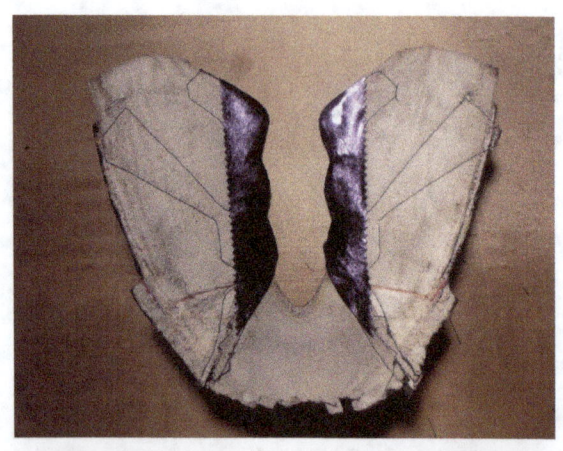

ANTHONY BOYD

Attach the heel box ends to the outer side ends on each sneaker only

HOW TO MAKE CUSTOM SEWN SNEAKERS

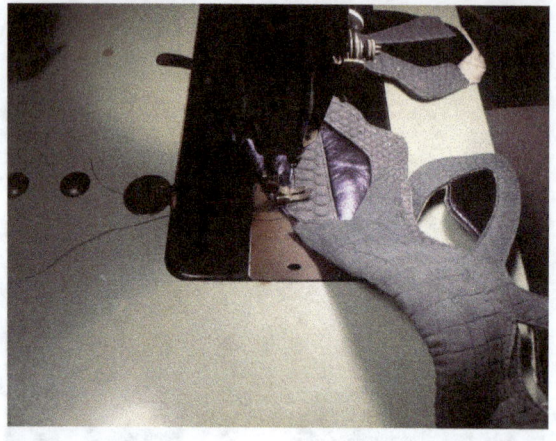

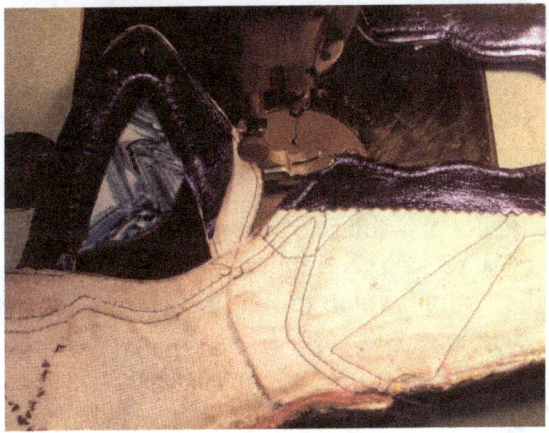

3a. Attach the upper ankle cushion side over the tip of the heel box where the outer sides meet

HOW TO MAKE CUSTOM SEWN SNEAKERS

Repeat the entire third step after you complete steps 5 & 5a (for the inner side on both sneakers)

4. Rebuild sock liners. Sort pieces into two piles, inside and outside pieces, then copy the toe portion by making a pattern from it. Then recreate the pieces on a fabric of your choice and sew it in place. Use the stay stitch to sew the outside pile and a straight stitch on the inside pile. Sew the inside and outside together at the upper top portion, then flip it onto the proper side, reglue the seams to hold it in place, and then stitch along the ends of the outside piece.

ANTHONY BOYD

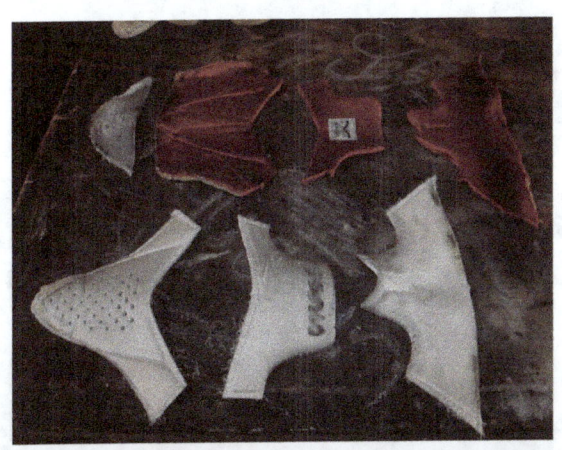

HOW TO MAKE CUSTOM SEWN SNEAKERS

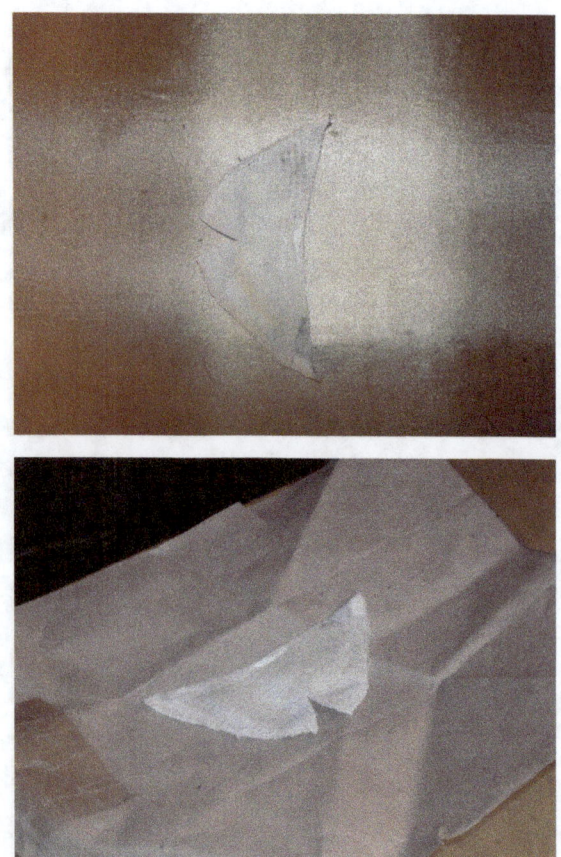

ANTHONY BOYD

HOW TO MAKE CUSTOM SEWN SNEAKERS

ANTHONY BOYD

HOW TO MAKE CUSTOM SEWN SNEAKERS

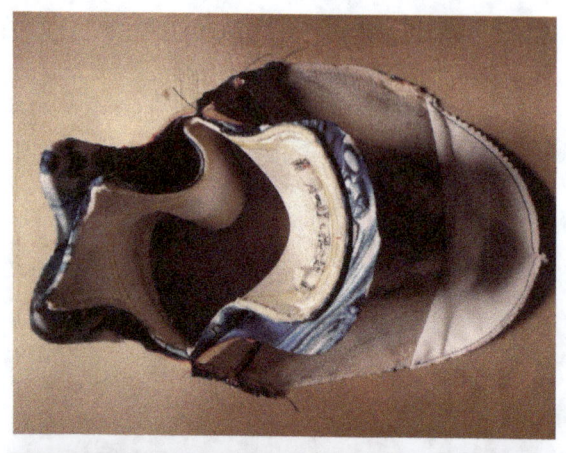

ANTHONY BOYD

5. Attach the pull tab to the back of the liner by sewing a box at the end of the tab.

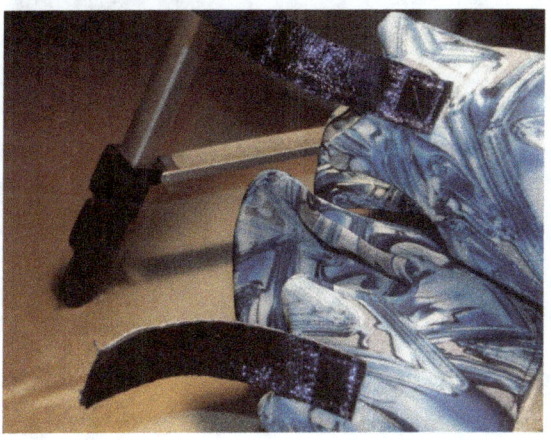

5a Sew the 23 patch to the heel box with the pull tab under it.

HOW TO MAKE CUSTOM SEWN SNEAKERS

5b Repeat the third step in its entirety and sew this section with the liner hanging out the back

ANTHONY BOYD

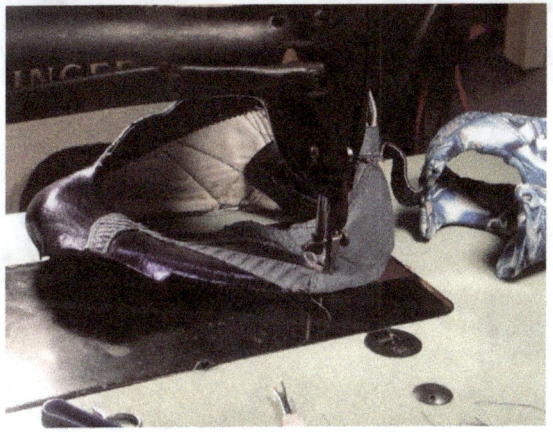

HOW TO MAKE CUSTOM SEWN SNEAKERS

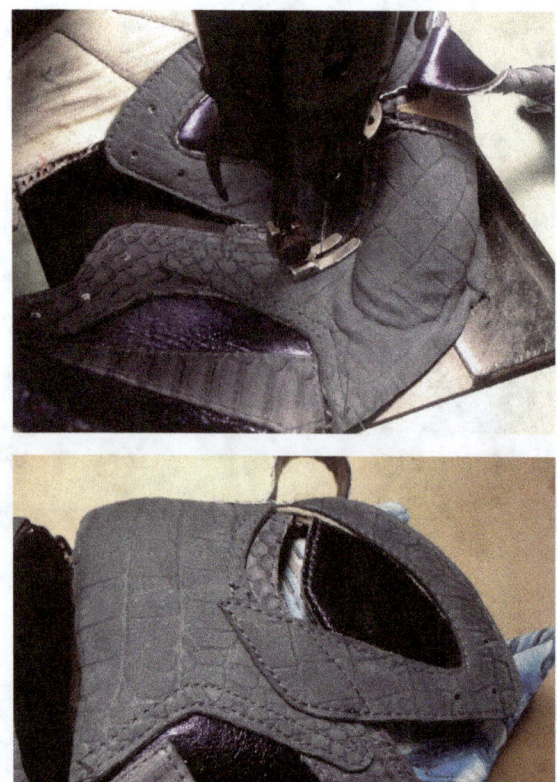

5c Pull the sock liner through and place a small amount of glue at the toe box where the lace-up begins, then stitch it in place to the sneaker.

ANTHONY BOYD

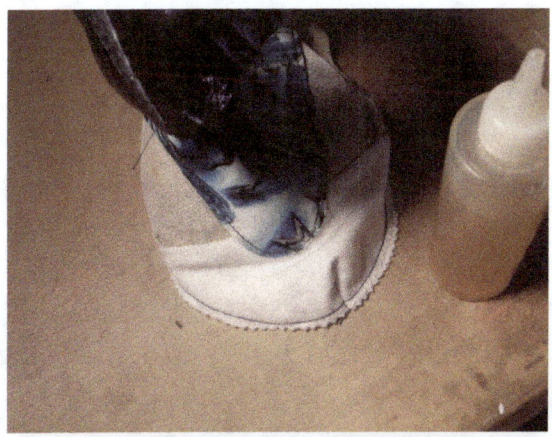

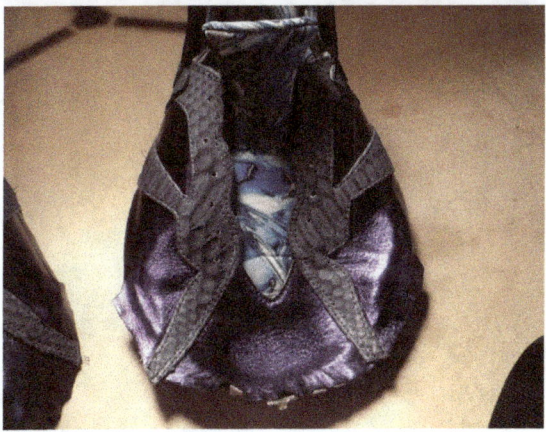

Shows how it should lie under the sewing machine

HOW TO MAKE CUSTOM SEWN SNEAKERS

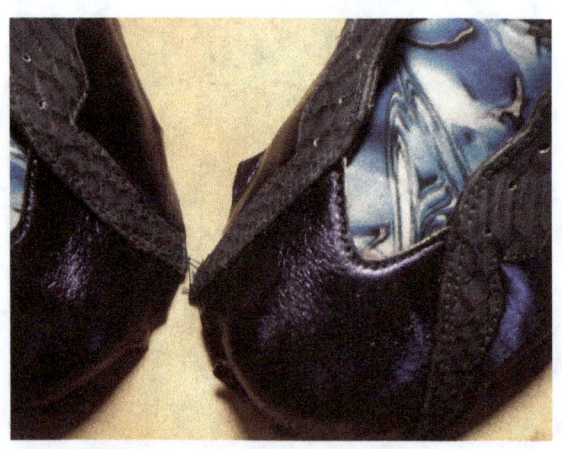

ANTHONY BOYD

Chapter 6:
Rebuilding the Foundation

SHOE LASTING/RUBBER CEMENT/CROSS STITCH FABRIC

A last is a mechanical form that has a shape similar to that of a human foot.

It is used by shoemakers and cordwainers in the manufacture and repair of shoes.

Lasts typically come in pairs and have been made from various materials, including hardwoods, cast iron, and high-density plastics.

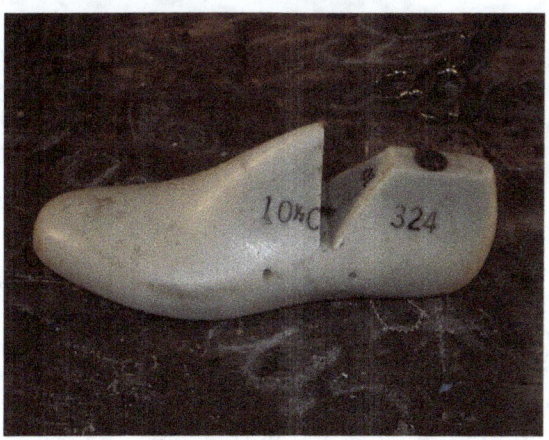

Rubber cement is an adhesive made from elastic

polymers (typically latex) mixed in a solvent such as acetone, hexane, heptane or toluene to keep them fluid enough to be used.

Water-based formulas, often stabilized by ammonia, are also available. This makes it part of the class of drying adhesives: As the solvents quickly evaporate, the "rubber" portion remains behind, forming a strong, yet flexible, bond.

Cross Stitch Fabric includes aida, linen and mixed-content fabrics called "evenweave."

All cross stitch fabrics are technically "evenweave." It refers to the fact that the fabric is woven to make sure that there are the same number of threads in an inch both left to right and top to bottom (vertically and horizontally). Fabrics are categorized by threads per inch (referred to as "count"), and can range from 11 to 40 count. For this project we will be using the 14 count weight.

OTHER TOOLS NEEDED: Hand Clamps, Rubber Mallet, Small Nails, Ruler, Elastic Bands, Hand Sewing Needle.

LASTING PREPARATION

These tools will be used to stabilize, shape and in some cases reform the sneaker, as well as assist in reattaching the under and outer sole.

Fit the toe box of the liner into the toe box of the sneaker with the lips for folding free of liner material.

HOW TO MAKE CUSTOM SEWN SNEAKERS

Cut a 2" x 13" strip out of suede and attach it to the shoe liner where the lips of the toe box begin, with the rough side up.

Then set the liner at the heel so that it's centered and flush so you can sew the strip along the bottom of the sneaker.

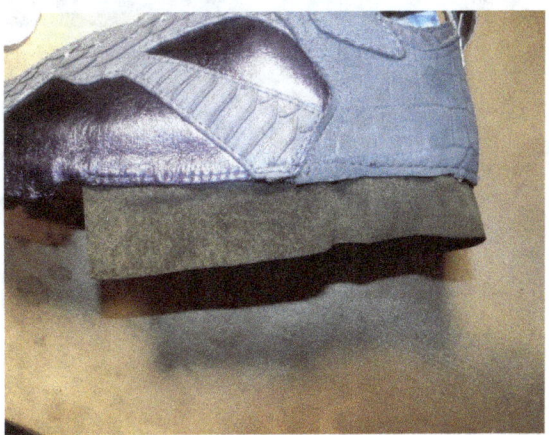

Trace the bottom of the last onto the cross-stitch fabric four times, then cut them out and glue tack

HOW TO MAKE CUSTOM SEWN SNEAKERS

them together. Stitch around the outside and double stitch a line 1/2" in from the outside stitch. Transfer markings from the under sole to your new under sole made of cross stitch fabric.

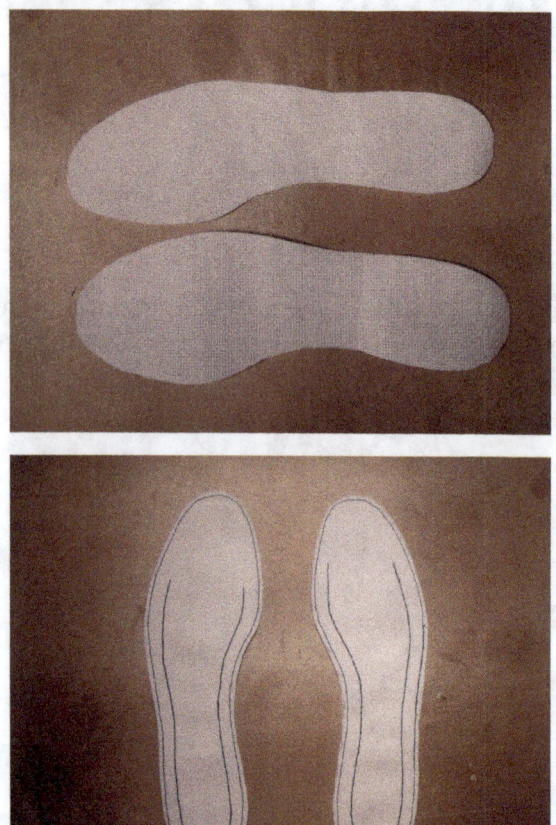

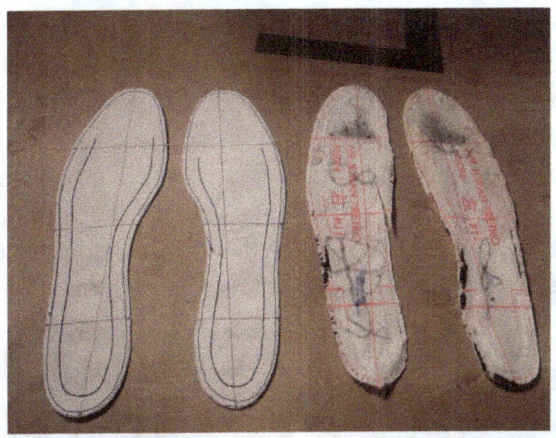

Place the under sole on the bottom of the last with spray glue, not a lot, just enough so it doesn't move while you're working.

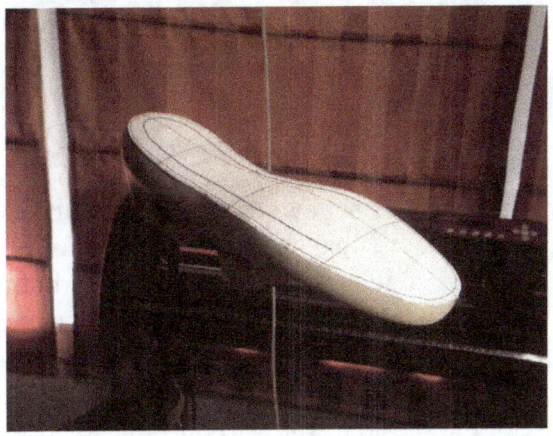

Put the sneaker on the last, making sure that the front and back center points of the sneaker fall

HOW TO MAKE CUSTOM SEWN SNEAKERS

directly down the center point of the front and back of the last. Make sure there is enough ease to fold over onto the under sole. You will see the natural line of the fold. You may need to nail the sneaker in place in order to complete the next step of folding and cementing. Be sure not to place the nails too low at the toe. If it holds, stop there. If not, nail sides but NOT too low.

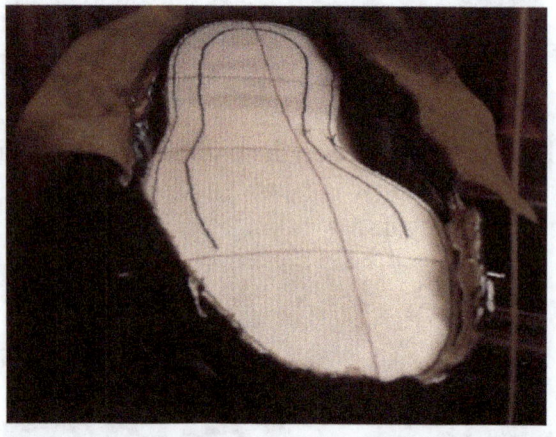

Apply rubber cement along the edges of the ease on the sneaker (lips). Your first coat is to ready the surface so it sticks, so let it dry some but not all the way. Do the same to the edges of the under sole where the ease will fold over to. Apply your second coat to both the under sole edge and the ease of the sneaker. Allow for the glue to become tacky before folding it over. Apply some pressure by hand and by using elastic straps and hand clamps to stabilize the position until you have a permanent bond. You can also pound the edges with a rubber mallet to flatten some areas.

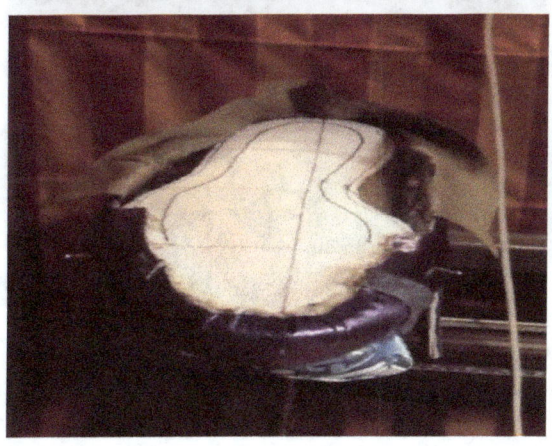

HOW TO MAKE CUSTOM SEWN SNEAKERS

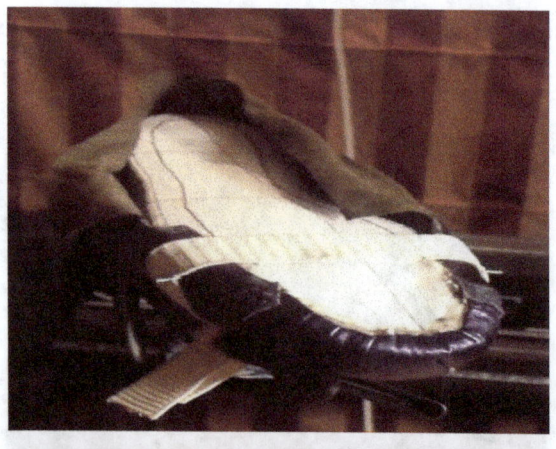

Now apply cement to the mid and heel portion of the under sole between the stitches and on the suede strip using the same glue methods as above. Pull firmly but gently and fold over the suede to the double stitched line all the way around. Apply some pressure by hand. and by using elastic straps and hand clamps to stabilize the position until you have a permanent bond. Allow 24 hrs for it to dry before proceeding to the next step.

HOW TO MAKE CUSTOM SEWN SNEAKERS

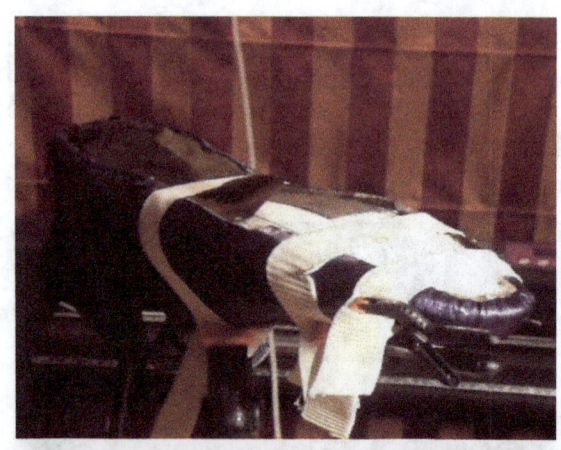

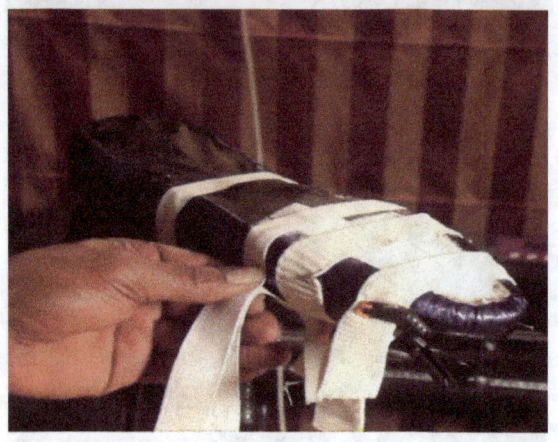

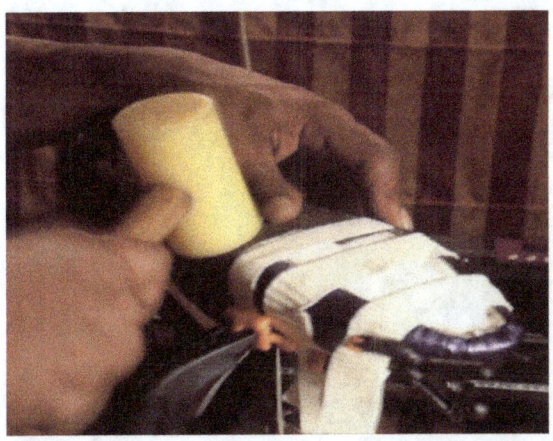

Cut away the excess fabric and begin hand sewing the suede to the double stitched line all the way around.

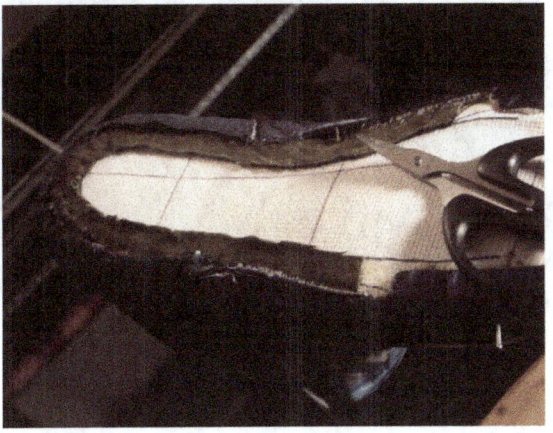

HOW TO MAKE CUSTOM SEWN SNEAKERS

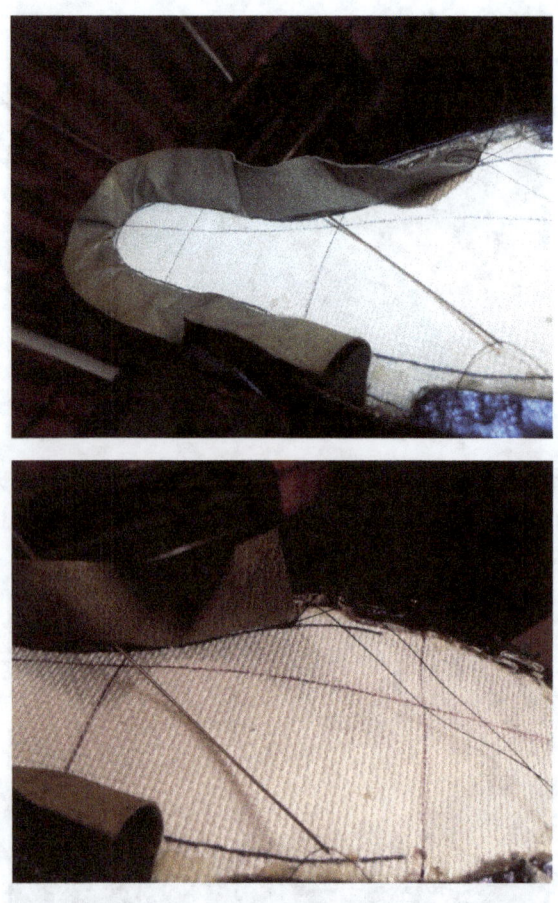

ANTHONY BOYD

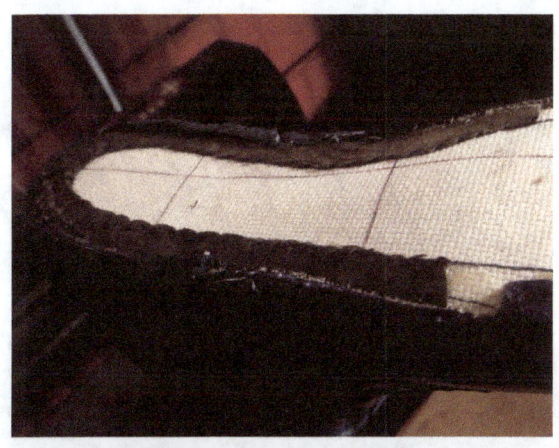

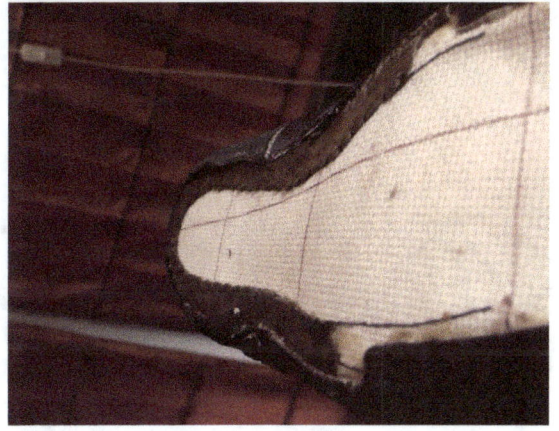

HOW TO MAKE CUSTOM SEWN SNEAKERS

Chapter 7:
Second Preparation

This is where you do any kind of prep work, during the time your under sole is bonding. You should allow at least 24 hrs of drying before going on to the next step of attaching the grip. Your grip should be free of any dirt, so clean the surface well. Now apply paint to the areas of your choice, and allow the paint time to dry properly according to the directions of your paint choice (curing time). Re-punch the lace holes if need be, and any other place where it's needed, removing the sneaker from the last if necessary.

HOW TO MAKE CUSTOM SEWN SNEAKERS

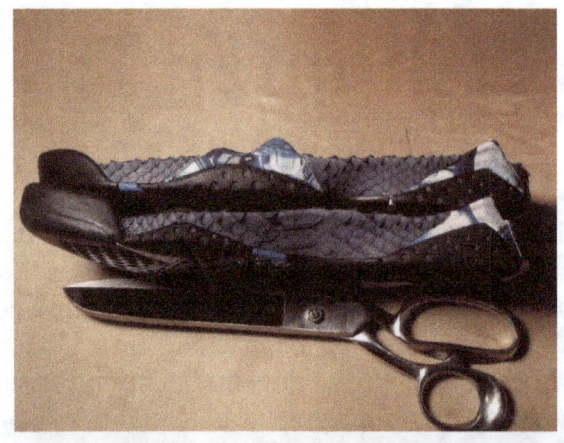

Covered grips

Chapter 8:
Reattaching the Grip

For reattaching the grip, you're going to need the following tools: RUBBER CEMENT, ELASTIC BANDS, HAND CLAMPS, AND A PAIR OF CALF-HIGH SOCKS (LOL, YEAH A PAIR OF SOCKS) (brand new because you're going to need the tightness of the knit).

Make sure the area you are applying rubber cement to is free of dirt. You're going to be applying at least three coats, using the coating method discussed in chapter 6, to the inner part of the grip and to the bottom of the sneaker on the last.

HOW TO MAKE CUSTOM SEWN SNEAKERS

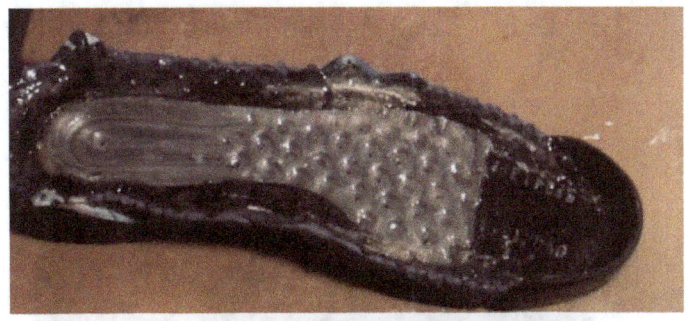

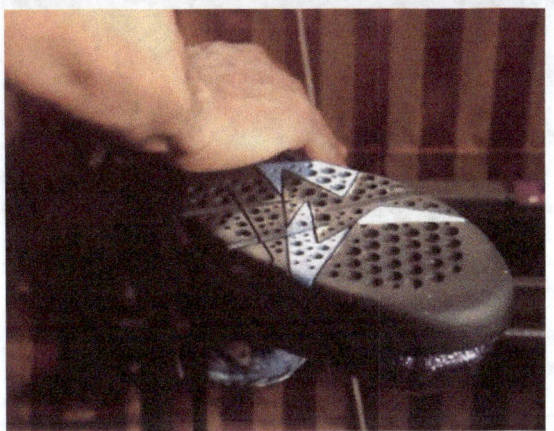

Allow both time to become very tacky before joining them together. Keep in mind to align the center front and the center back of the lasted sneaker and the center front and the center back of the grip before joining them.

Once joined, pressure needs to be applied. Usually in this case a soling machine would be used to create the even pressure needed to join them correctly. I found that elastic bands work well in creating even pressure so spread them out and apply as many as needed to stabilize the grip and lasted sneaker.

The Sock Ends create even pressure for the ball

of the last, the area on the foot where it bends. You will notice the curve in the last as you attach the grip and how it cuffs at the bend. Your first elastic band will stabilize the center only but not the sides of that area.

Roll the sock up as if you were putting them on and slide them over the sneaker so the double knit surrounds the toe.

HOW TO MAKE CUSTOM SEWN SNEAKERS

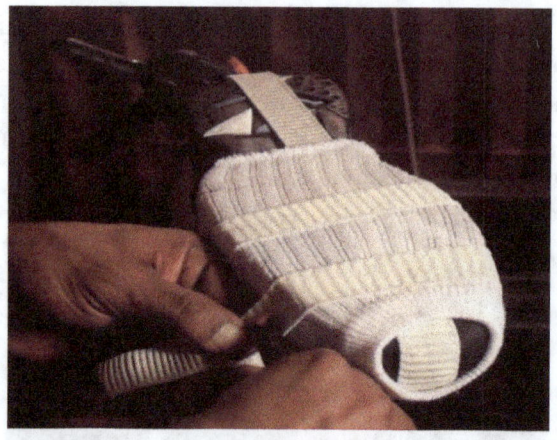

Begin adding elastic bands to create even more pressure.

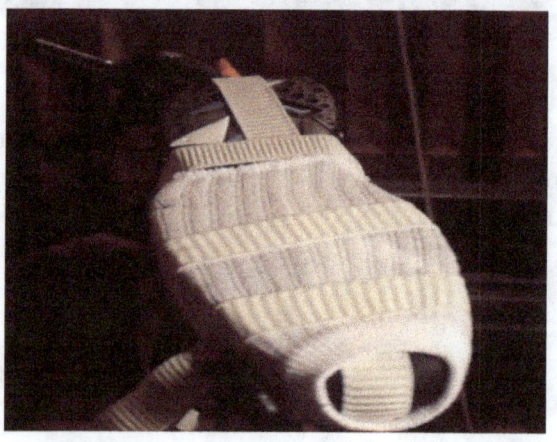

ANTHONY BOYD

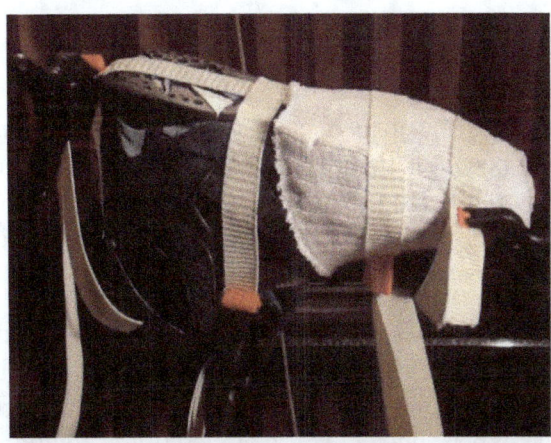

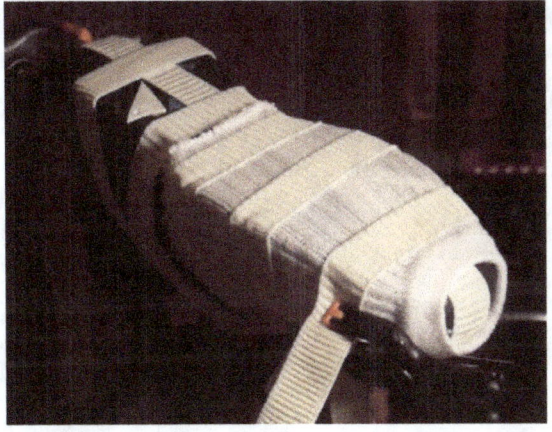

Allow the sneaker 24 hours to dry before removing the bands. Check where the sneaker and grip meet all the way around for bonding and apply cement to areas that may have not stuck completely. Then you may have to clean up any loose glue by rolling it away or by brushing it with a

HOW TO MAKE CUSTOM SEWN SNEAKERS

suede brush.

Remove the sneaker from the last and begin sewing, into the grip if needed. It should be fairly easy because the holes in the sneaker will guide you if lined up properly. The center front and back the holes in the sneaker should line up with the holes in the grip.

Visit Us @ www.anaghe.com to preview the finish pair (The Blue Print) and to watch the step by step instructional videos to increase your learning experience . These videos are available ONLY to Book buyers and Members of Anaghe&Co. And be sure to inquire about our 1 on 1 classes in the members section. Thank You So Much for this purchase & may God Bless your hands to create the desires of your heart !

THE END

www.ingramcontent.com/pod-product-compliance
Lightning Source LLC
Chambersburg PA
CBHW072104290426
44110CB00014B/1812